Blood Brothers

D0541342

Willy Russell

Introduction and notes by
Chas White
and Chris Shepherd

BELL BAXTER HIGH SCHOOL
WEST PORT
CUPAR

RECEIVED
- 4 SEP 1990

STUDIO SCRIPTS

Stanley Thornes (Publishers) Ltd

© Willy Russell 1986
Introduction and notes © Chas White and Chris Shepherd

All rights reserved. No part of this publication may be reproduced or
transmitted in any form or by any means, electronic or mechanical,
including photocopy, recording, or any information storage and retrieval
system, without permission in writing from the publisher or under
licence from the Copyright Licensing Agency Limited. Further details of
such licences (for reprographic reproduction) may be obtained from the
Copyright Licensing Agency Limited, of 33–4 Alfred Place, London
WC1E 7DP.

Originally published in 1986 by Hutchinson Education
Reprinted 1987, 1988

Reprinted in 1989 by
Stanley Thornes (Publishers) Ltd
Old Station Drive
Leckhampton
CHELTENHAM GL53 0DN

British Library Cataloguing in Publication Data

Russell, Willy
   Blood brothers.—(Studio scripts)
   I. Title   II. Harman, Paul   III. Series
   822'.914   PR6068.U86

   ISBN 0 7487 0182 6

*Cover picture shows l. Eddie (Andrew C. Wadsworth)
and r. Mickey (George Costigan) in the West End
production of* Blood Brothers.

Set in Century Schoolbook by
Words & Pictures Ltd, Thornton Heath, Surrey

Printed and bound in Great Britain at
The Bath Press, Avon.

Contents

Introduction   7

The Writer   9

Presenting the Play   10

The First Performance   11

Blood Brothers   13

Follow-up Activities   74

All rights whatsoever in this play are strictly reserved and application for professional performance should be made before rehearsal to Margaret Ramsay Ltd, 14A Goodwin's Court, St Martin's Lane, London WC2N 4LL.

Application for amateur performance should be made to Samuel French Ltd, 52 Fitzroy Street, London W1P 6JR.

STUDIO SCRIPTS

Series editor: David Self

Situation Comedy
Situation Comedy 2
Love and Marriage
School
Scully *Alan Bleasdale*
Boys from the Blackstuff *Alan Bleasdale*
Blood Brothers *Willy Russell*
Radio Scripts

Introduction

This play, which was written for Merseyside Young People's Theatre Company, takes as its starting point a traditional idea in literature – the separation of twins at birth – but it handles this idea in a very modern way. Mrs Johnston is a working-class Liverpudlian, a deserted wife with seven children who is again pregnant, with twins, at the beginning of the play. She cleans for the middle-class Mrs Lyons with whom she contrasts strongly, and not just because Mrs Lyons cannot have children but will not admit this to her husband. Mrs Lyons suggests that one twin be given to her so that the child could grow up and 'have everything'. She reinforces her point: 'Surely, surely, Mrs Johnston it's better to give one child to me than to have some of them taken into care.'

So the play is centred on twins who are inextricably linked in this way by birth yet separated by background and upbringing. Mrs Lyons becomes determined that the two boys should not meet or associate, but fate intervenes. Eddie and Mickey meet and ironically swear to become blood brothers. Although their liking for each other prevails at first, their contrasting environments force them apart. Tragedy occurs because their upbringing prevents a proper understanding of each other.

The episodic nature of the play allows Willy Russell to focus on the degree to which success in life is determined not by innate qualities but by the privileges, or disadvantages, of our upbringing. This pervasive inequality is dramatized in the contrasting fortunes of the blood brothers.

The play considers family, education, employment, housing, and relationships and offers not only entertainment but also a great number of topics and starting points for discussion, improvization and writing on concerns relevant to young people today.

The play is a mixture of styles. Within each scene costume and acting are naturalistic, but *Blood Brothers* also has the variety of non-naturalistic drama: it is a musical, smaller parts are all played by the same person, there is a narrator, sets and props are kept to the bare essentials. All of these features make it appropriate for performance in schools (its first performance was at Fazakerley Comprehensive on Merseyside), and in clubs and halls which attract audiences of non-regular theatregoers. The cast is small with a good balance of strong male and female roles. This version of the play is not the musical one.

This is the original drama script written for performance in schools by Merseyside Young People's Theatre Company. However the publishers suggest that due to the nature of some of the language in the play some teachers might prefer to check through the play before using it with young people.

The Writer

Willy Russell

Willy Russell was born just outside Liverpool, and at the age of 5 moved to Knowsley. His father owned a chip shop and his mother worked in a warehouse. Academically he was a failure at school but it was during English silent reading lessons that he realized he wanted to be a writer.

He left school with an English Language O level as his only qualification to work for six years as a hairdresser. He then took English Literature at evening class, and having passed that decided to go to college for a year. In order to pay the fees for this he worked at the dangerous but well paid job of night-shift girder cleaner at Fords.

Among his other plays Willy Russell has written 'John, Paul, George, Ringo and Bert' and 'Educating Rita'. Other plays by Willy Russell published by Stanley Thornes are 'Our Day Out' in *Act One*, 'Lies' in *Studio Scripts: City Life*, 'The Boy with the Transistor Radio' in *Studio Scripts: Working* and 'Politics and Terror' in *Wordplays 1*.

Presenting the Play

In class

The most informal classroom reading of a playscript is helped by rehearsal. Even a very experienced professional actor prefers to look over his or her part before a first reading in front of his or her colleagues. In the classroom too, those who will be reading should be given time to look over their lines: to make sure that they know when to pause, when to 'interrupt' the previous speech, and to work out the changing mood of their character before they are asked to read aloud.

It is much easier to read effectively and convincingly from a standing position or from one where you can be seen by your audience. It may be helpful to appoint a 'director' who will decide the location of various settings and rehearse the actors in basic movements, checking that they know when and where to enter and exit.

Note that it is possible for a class to break up into groups, and for each of these to rehearse its own interpretation of one or more scenes, and then present their readings in turn to the whole class.

On stage

See Paul Harman's description of the original production on the opposite page.

The First Performance

Blood Brothers was commissioned by Merseyside Young People's Theatre Company with the aid of a Contract Writer's Award from the Arts Council of Great Britain. MYPT is financially assisted by Merseyside Arts to provide a subsidized service of theatre of the highest quality for young people in schools on Merseyside.

The first performance, of sixty in secondary schools in the region, was at Fazakerley Comprehensive on 9 November 1981.

The Director was Paul Harman

The original production was designed for playing on the floor of a school hall to an optimum audience of 120. Chairs were arranged on all four sides of a square leaving room for access at each corner. A chair, a table, a pram and a small packing case were used with small props where essential. Each scene change and the interventions of the **Narrator** were marked by freezes and the sound of claves (wooden sticks knocked together), and we used vocalized birdsong, machine noises etc. as appropriate. Costume and acting style within scenes were naturalistic.

Paul Harman

Mrs Johnston (Barbara Dickson) in the West End production of Blood Brothers

Blood Brothers

Characters

Eddie   ⎤ twin brothers
Mickey   ⎦
The Mother (Mrs Johnston), their real mother
Mrs Lyons, who adopts Eddie
Linda, friend of Mickey and Eddie
Narrator
Milkman
Doctor
Policewoman
Chorus   including   Kid One
                       Kid Two
                       Kid Three
                       Kid Four

Act 1, scene 1

Narrator: [*Idiomatic rather than BBC*]
So did you ever hear the tale of the Johnston twins,
As like each other as two new pins;
Of one womb born, on the self same day,
How one was kept, one given away?

Did you ever hear tell of that young mother
Who stood and watched brother parted from brother;
Who saw her children wrenched apart,
That woman, with a stone in place of a heart?

Then bring her on, come on let's see
The author of such cruelty.
And judge for ourselves this terrible sin.
Bring on the mother, let the story begin.

[**The Mother** *enters. She's thirty, but looks sixty. The rest of the cast, including the* **Narrator** *lay down a vocal backing reminiscent of the Ink Spots/Four Preps. Very ritzy harmony, enjoying themselves and their routine.* **The Mother** *sings extremely directly and matter of factly, almost in contrast to her backing*]

The Mother:
Once I had a husband
You know the sort of chap.
I met him at a dance and how he came on with the chat.
He said my eyes were deep blue pools
My skin as soft as snow
He told me I was sexier
Than Marilyn Monroe
And we went dancing

Chorus: Bob bob a bob bob bob a bob

Chorus/The Mother: Oh we went dancing

The Mother:

Then of course I found
That I was six weeks overdue
We got married at the registry and then we had a do.
We all had curly salmon sandwiches
And how the ale did flow;
They said the bride was lovelier
Than Marilyn Monroe
And we went dancing

Chorus: [*as before*] Oh we went dancing

The Mother:

Then the baby came along
We called him Darren Wayne
Then three months on I found that I was in the club
    again
And though I still fancied dancing
My husband wouldn't go
With a wife he said
Was twice the size
Of Marilyn Monroe
No more dancing

Chorus: [*as before*] No more dancing

The Mother:

By the time that I was twenty-five
I looked like forty-two
With seven hungry mouths to feed and one more nearly
    due
Me husband had walked out on me
A month or two ago
For a girl, they say
Who looks a bit like Marilyn Monroe
And they go dancing

Chorus: [*as before*]
Yes they go dancing

Oh they go dancing, yes they go dancing . . .

[*The Backers and* **The Mother** *go into a little step routine.* **The Mother** *turns invitingly to one of the Backers, expecting him to dance, but he rudely cuts into the melody and lays a milkman's hat on his head*]

Act 1, scene 2

Milkman: I've had enough of your hard luck story, love.

The Mother: Look, honest, I will pay you next week. I know I've said . . .

Milkman: But next week never comes as far as you're concerned, love. With you it's always next week.

The Mother: But I start a job next week. I'll have money coming in. I'll be able to pay you. You can't stop the milk. I need the milk. I'm pregnant.

Milkman: Well don't look at me, love. I might be the milkman but it's nothing to do with me. No money, no milk!

[**The Mother** *stands staring as he rejoins the* **Chorus**, *removing his milkman's hat. The* **Chorus** *become the voices of kids*]

Kid One: Mam, the baby's crying. He wants a bottle. Where's the milk?

Kid Two: How come I'm on free dinners, Mam. All the other kids laugh at me.

Kid Three: Hey, mother, I'm starving. There's nothing in.

Kid Four: Mum . . . mum, there's no bread. Mum, I can't sleep. I'm hungry.

The Mother: [*Singing, alone*]

I know it's hard on all you kids
But try and get some sleep,
Next week I'll be earning, there'll be loads of stuff
    to eat.
There'll be mince and spuds and bread
And cakes when I bring home the dough
We'll live like kings
Like bright young things,
Like Marilyn Monroe
And we'll go dancing . . .
We'll go dancing . . .

[*She hums a few bars of the tune and dances*]

Act 1, scene 3

As she dances she acquires brush and dusters and mop bucket and the scene changes into a working situation. **The Mother** *busily working and humming the melody.* **Mrs Lyons** *(her employer) enters. Bright, breezy, early thirties. She carries a small parcel.*

Mrs Lyons: Hello, Mrs Johnston. How are you? How are you enjoying the job?

The Mother: Oh it's, it's smashing thank you, Mrs Lyons. It's such a lovely house it's a pleasure to clean it.

Mrs Lyons: Yes, it's a pretty house isn't it? It's a pity it's so big. I'm finding it rather large at present.

The Mother: Oh with Mr Lyons being away and that, yeh. When does he get back, Mrs Lyons?

Mrs Lyons: Oh, let me see, the company sent him out for nine months, that means, what, he'll be back in about five months.

The Mother: Ah. You'll be glad won't you? The house will feel empty until he's back.

Mrs Lyons: [*Beginning to unwrap the parcel as* **The Mother** *continues cleaning*] Actually Mrs J we bought such a large house for the children. We thought children were going to come along.

The Mother: You can't have any?

Mrs Lyons: No, I'm afraid ... I wanted to adopt but Mr Lyons is, well ... He says he always wanted his own son, not someone else's. Myself I believe that an adopted child can become one's own.

The Mother: Ah yeh ... yeh. It's weird isn't it? Here's you can't have kids and me, I can't stop having them. Me husband used to say that all we had to do was shake hands and I'd be in the club again. I'm expecting another one you know.

Mrs Lyons: Ah ...

The Mother: Oh but look, look, it's all right ... I'll still be able to do me work. Having babies, it's like clockwork to me. I'm back on me feet and working the next day. If I have it at the weekend I won't even need to take one day off. I love this job you know. And we can just get by now you know. Well I'll go and do the bathroom now and ... [*She is stopped as* **Mrs Lyons** *puts the new shoes from the parcel she has unwrapped on to the table*] Oh Jesus Christ ... Mrs Lyons, Mrs, What are you doing?

Mrs Lyons: What's wrong, here sit down, what's wrong?

The Mother: [*Pointing*] The shoes, the shoes ...

Mrs Lyons: What's wrong with them?

The Mother: On ... on the table. Take them off ... take them off!

[**Mrs Lyons** *does so*]

The Mother: [*Relieved*] Oh God. Never put new shoes on a table, Mrs Lyons. You never know what'll happen.

Mrs Lyons: [*Twigging, laughing*] Oh, you mean it's superstition. You're superstitious are you?

The Mother: No. But you never put new shoes on a table.

Mrs Lyons: Oh go on with you. If it will make you happier I shall put them away.

[*She exits.* **The Mother** *approaches the table, wary. She half absently rubs the spot on which the shoes were standing*]

Narrator:
There's shoes on the table, a joker in the pack,
The salt was spilled and the mirror's cracked
There's one lone magpie overhead
And I'm not superstitious, the mother said.
No I'm not superstitious, the mother said.

Act 1, scene 4

Immediately, the actor who played the **Milkman** *enters.*

The Mother: What are you doing here? The milk bill's not due till Friday. I don't owe you anything.

Doctor: [*Whipping out a listening funnel*] Actually I've given up the milk round and gone into medicine! I'm your gynaecologist now! [*He places the funnel on her belly, to listen to the baby's heartbeat*] OK, Mummy, let's have a little listen to baby's ticker, shall we?

The Mother: [*As the* **Gynaecologist** *shifts from position to position, making knowing noises*] I was dead worried about having another mouth to feed you know doctor. But I'll be all right now. I've got a little job. If I'm careful we can just scrape by, even if there is going to be another mouth to feed.

Doctor: [*Putting away his funnel and preparing to leave*] 'Mouths', Mrs Johnston.

The Mother: Eh?

Doctor: Plural. Mouths. You're going to have twins! Congratulations!

[*He exits as* **Mrs Lyons** *enters to find* **The Mother** *dusting the table*]

Act 1, scene 5

Mrs Lyons: Hello, Mrs J. You're here early, aren't you?

The Mother: I had it all worked out. We were just getting straight. With one more baby we could have managed. But not with two. The Welfare's already been on to me. They say I'm incapable of controlling the kids I've already got. They say I should put some of them into care. But I won't. Because I love them. I love the bones of every one of them. I'll even love these two twins. But like they say at the Welfare, kids can't live on love alone.

Mrs Lyons: You're expecting twins?

[*The women freeze as:*]

Narrator: [*Setting Bible on table*]
How quickly an idea planted can
Take root and grow into a plan.
A thought conceived in this very room
Grew as surely as a seed, in a mother's womb!

The Mother: Give one of them to you?

Mrs Lyons: Yes. Yes!

The Mother: But I've ... how the ...

Mrs Lyons: When are you due?

The Mother: Erm, well I think it's the ... but, Mrs Lyons, what ...

Mrs Lyons: Quickly, quickly, tell me when you're due?

The Mother: About, about December the fifteenth ...

Mrs Lyons: [*A gasp of joy*] One week before my husband gets back. He need never guess. Look, look, you're five months pregnant but you're only just beginning to show. Look [*Grabs a small shawl and arranges it below her dress*] I'm only just beginning to show. I could have just got pregnant before he went away. I didn't tell him in case I miscarried, I didn't want him to worry while he was away. But, when he arrives home, I tell him, the doctors were wrong, I have a baby, our baby. Look [*Her 'pregnancy'*] Oh Mrs Johnston, Mrs Johnston, it will work, I know it will ...

The Mother: But look, I don't know if ...

Mrs Lyons: You said yourself, you said you had too many children.

The Mother: I know, but I don't know if I want to give one away.

Mrs Lyons: Already you're being threatened by the Welfare. With two more how will you avoid some of them being put into care? Surely, surely, Mrs Johnston, it's better to give one child to me than to have some of them taken into care! If he's with me you'll still be able to see him each day as you come to work.

[**Mrs Lyons** *gives her a moment in which to think.* **The Mother,** *anxious, chewing her bottom lip, turning and looking around her*]

The Mother: He'd ... he'd have a good life if he grew up here wouldn't he? I'd still have the other one. And you do want a baby, don't you? [**Mrs Lyons** *nodding*] He'd be able to play on those lawns wouldn't he? And have his own room and ...

Mrs Lyons: If he grew up here ... as our son ... He could have everything.

[**The Mother** *stares and thinks.* **Mrs Lyons** *hardly dares breathe. Eventually almost imperceptibly,* **The Mother** *nods*]

Mrs Lyons: Yes?

The Mother: Yeh.

Mrs Lyons: [*A gasp*] Oh ... Mrs Johnston ... I could dance. [*Indeed she does a few steps, waltzing* **The Mother** *who, inhibited and slightly embarrassed, laughs at this expression of joy*]

The Mother: Oh hey, Mrs Lyons, ... you are a case!

Mrs Lyons: [*Suddenly stopping, swiftly changing key*] But no one must ever know. Certificates can be arranged. I can pay. No one must ever know. Do you agree?

The Mother: Well ... if ...

Mrs Lyons: [*Grabbing a Bible*] Put your hand on this ...

The Mother: But ...

Mrs Lyons: We have to do it like this, Mrs Johnston. We have to ... Say these words ... 'At the birth of my twins ...'

The Mother: At er ...

Mrs Lyons: Yes, go on, go on ... at the birth of my twins ...

The Mother: At the birth of my twins, oh, I can't do ...

Mrs Lyons: Come on, come on, you know it's for the best.

'At the birth of my twins I shall give one of the children to Jennifer J. Lyons'

The Mother: I shall give one of the children to Jennifer J. Lyons . . .

Mrs Lyons: And renounce all further claim on the said child . . .

The Mother: And, and renounce all claim on, all further claim on the said child . . .

Mrs Lyons: [*Removing the Bible*] Good . . . good.

[**The Mother** *watches as* **Mrs Lyons** *goes to a mirror and attends to the shawl beneath her dress. She looks at the result and is obviously pleased with the effect*]

The Mother: I will be able to see him every day, won't I?

Mrs Lyons: Mm? Oh yes, of course.

The Mother: I don't suppose it's really giving one away is it? I mean it'll just be like he's living in another house, won't it?

Mrs Lyons: Yes . . . yes [*Turning and displaying her 'pregnancy'*] What do you think? Does it look right?

The Mother: Well it is a bit high for five months.

[**The Mother** *moves across and attends to the shawl in order better to suggest mid-term pregnancy*]

Mrs Lyons: Do you know, it's almost as though I can feel the child growing inside me.

The Mother: It's only a shawl.

Mrs Lyons: [*Brushing her away*] I'm going to the shops.

The Mother: I always do the shopping.

Mrs Lyons: No. No, I want to do the shopping from now on.

[*She exits, holding her belly proudly before her.* **The Mother** *stands, staring and thinking, absently touching the table and, with her other hand, her belly*]

Act 1, scene 6

Narrator: [*As* **The Mother** *turns and begins to attend to a twin cot*]
How quickly those who've made a pact
Can come to overlook the fact.
Oh that the reckoning could be delayed
But a debt is a debt. And must be paid.

[**The Mother**, *bright and cheerful, fussing over the cots, when suddenly there is an extremely loud and insistent knocking on the door.* **The Mother** *startled, apprehensive. She turns as* **Mrs Lyons**, *now fully 'pregnant', enters and glares at her. She sees the cot*]

Mrs Lyons: They're born? You didn't notify me!

The Mother: Well I didn't . . . I just . . . it's . . . couldn't I keep them, just for a few more days. Please, I mean they seem to be such a perfect pair, they sort of go together and if . . .

Mrs Lyons: My husband is due back tomorrow! I must have my baby now. You agreed, Mrs Johnston. Look. [*Produces the Bible*] We made a bargain. You made a promise!

The Mother: [*Knowing it's futile, turning away, back to the cots*] You'd better see which one you want.

Mrs Lyons: [*Cautiously approaches the cots. She lets out a tiny gasp of excitement as she peers in*] Oh. [*She ponders a moment*] I'll take the one with . . .

The Mother: Don't tell me. Don't tell me which one. Just take him.

[**Mrs Lyons** *rapidly pulls out the padding beneath her dress. Among this padding is a shawl which she wraps around the baby before lifting it from the cot. She hurries to the door*]

Mrs Lyons: I'll erm ... I'll see you next week.

The Mother: [*Without turning*] I'm due back tomorrow.

Mrs Lyons: Why ... erm why don't you take the week off? On full pay of course.

[**The Mother** *slowly nods as behind her* **Mrs Lyons** *exits*]

Act 1, scene 7

The Mother *turns and goes to her remaining twin. The remaining company become the voices of the kids.*

Kid One: Where's the other twinny, Mam?

The Mother: Gone to live with your Aunty in America. She'll look after him. We couldn't afford to keep him here. Not the two of them love.

Kid Two: Have we got an Aunty in America?

The Mother: Yeh.

Kid Two: Ooh ... can I go?

The Mother: Huh. I'd take you today, love. But I've got to go to work.

Act 1, scene 8

The Mother *turns to talk to the baby in the cot as* **Mrs Lyons** *enters.*

The Mother: Ah he's really coming on now isn't he, Mrs Lyons? I'll bet Mr Lyons is dead proud of him, isn't he?

Mrs Lyons: Yes. Yes he is.

The Mother: Ah he's lovely . . . Look he wants to be picked up. I'll just . . .

Mrs Lyons: No. No! It's all right, Mrs Johnston. He's fine. He doesn't want to be picked up.

The Mother: Ah but look he's . . .

Mrs Lyons: If he needs picking up I shall pick him up.

The Mother: Ah look he must be wet. [*Goes to pick up child.* **Mrs Lyons** *intervenes*]

Mrs Lyons: Leave him! Just . . . Just leave him. You're always . . . always bothering him, fussing over him.

The Mother: I'm sorry I just . . .

Mrs Lyons: Yes I know . . . I know what you're doing but you won't because Edward is my son. Mine, Mrs Johnston.

The Mother: Well I know, I just . . .

Mrs Lyons: Mr Lyons and I have been talking it over, Mrs Johnston, and we both think it would be better if you left.

The Mother: What? Left where?

Mrs Lyons: Your work has deteriorated. We're just not happy with it.

The Mother: But, but I work the way I've always worked.

Mrs Lyons: Yes, well I'm sorry, I'm not satisfied.

The Mother: What will I do? How are we going to live without me job?

Mrs Lyons: Yes, I've thought of that. Here . . . here's . . . [*Pushes the money into the hands of the stunned* **Mother**] It's a lot of money. But, but we don't want you to suffer.

The Mother: [*Thinking, desperate, trying to get it together*] OK. All right Mrs Lyons. Right. If I'm going, right . . . well well I'm taking Edward with me . . . I'm taking my son. [*She* *goes to the cot but is roughly dragged away*]

Mrs Lyons: Oh no you're not! Edward is my son!

The Mother: I'll tell someone . . . I'll tell the police . . . I'll bring the police in and . . .

Mrs Lyons: No you won't. You gave your baby away. Don't you realize what a crime that is? You sold your baby.

[**The Mother**, *horrified, throwing the wad of notes from her*]

The Mother: I didn't, I didn't . . . You told me . . . You said . . . you said I could see him every day. Well I'll tell someone . . . I'm going to tell . . .

[*As she tries to exit she is stopped by* **Mrs Lyons** *grabbing her and wheeling her about*]

Mrs Lyons: Oh no you will not. Because, because if you tell anyone, and these children learn of the truth then you know what will happen, don't you? You know what they say about twins secretly parted, don't you?

The Mother: [*Terrified*] What, what?

Mrs Lyons: They say . . . they say that if either twin learns he was one of a pair they shall both die immediately! It means, Mrs Johnston, that these brothers shall grow up unaware of the other's existence. They shall be raised apart, and never, never ever told what was once the truth. You won't tell anyone, Mrs Johnston, because if you do you shall kill them!

[**Mrs Lyons** *grabs the money and thrusts it into* **The Mother**'s *hands.* **Mrs Lyons**, *breathing heavily, relieved.* **The Mother**, *shocked.* **Mrs Lyons** *exits as the* **Narrator** *enters*]

Act 2, scene 1

[*Seven years later*]

Narrator:
There's no use clutching at your rosary
The Devil's in the backyard, he can see
Through the gaps in the curtains he sees it all,
There's no use hiding in the hall.
When he raps at the knocker then he knows you're in;
No you won't, no you'll never get away from him
No you won't, no you'll never get away from him.

[**The Narrator** *repeats the last line at* **The Mother**, *building in volume until he is stopped by a loud knocking at the door and* **The Mother** *screaming. She stares, horrified as the incessant knocking continues and then we hear a child's voice, off*]

Mickey: Mother. Will you open the bleeding door or what?

The Mother: [*Realizing it is only* **Mickey**. *Drained, relieved*] Mickey?

Mickey: [*Seven years old, enters carrying a toy gun*] Mum. [*She grabs him and hugs him to her*] What's up, Mam? Did you think I was the rent man? [**The Mother** *laughing and looking at him*] Mam our Sammy's robbed me other gun and that was me best one. Why does he rob all me things off me?

The Mother: Because you're the youngest Mickey. It used to happen to Sammy when he was the youngest.

Mickey: We're playing mounted Police, and Indians. I'm a Mountie. Mam, Mam, you know this morning we've wiped out three thousand Indians.

The Mother: Good!

Mickey: [*Aims the gun at her and 'fires'*] You're dead, Mam.

The Mother: [*Staring at him*] Hmm.

Mickey: Mam. What's wrong, Mam?

The Mother: Nothing, son. Go on, you go out and play. There's a good lad. But hey, don't you go playing down the rough end with those hooligans.

Mickey: I'm not. We're playing up the other end. Near the big houses in the park . . . [*He is about to go*]

The Mother: Mickey . . . come here

Mickey: [*Returning*] What?

The Mother: Where? Where have you been playing?

Mickey: Mam, Mam I'm sorry, I forgot.

The Mother: What have I told you about playing up near there, eh? [*She grabs him*]

Mickey: It wasn't my fault, honest.

The Mother: So whose fault was it?

Mickey: It was, it was . . . it was the Indians! They rode up that way, trying to escape.

The Mother: Don't you ever go up there. Do you hear me?

Mickey: Yeh. You let our Sammy go up there.

The Mother: Our Sammy's older than you.

Mickey: But why . . .

The Mother: Just shuttup. Never mind why. You don't go near there.

Mickey: You used to work up there, didn't you Mam?

The Mother: Yeh.

Mickey: When?

The Mother: Before you were born. Now go on. Get out

and play. But you stay outside the front door where I can
see you.

Mickey: Ah but, Mam, the ...

The Mother: Go on!

[**The Mother** *exits as* **Mickey** *makes his way outside. He is
fed up. Desultory, he shoots a few imaginary Indians but
somehow the magic has gone out of genocide. He sits, bored
and restless*]

Mickey:

I wish I was our Sammy.
Our Sammy's nearly ten.
He's got two worms and a catapault
And he's built an underground den.
But I'm not allowed to go in there.
I have to stay near the gate.
Me Mam says I'm only seven;
But I'm not, I'm nearly eight!

I wish I was our Sammy,
You want to see him spit!
Straight in your eye from twenty yards,
And every time, a hit.
He's allowed to play with matches
And he goes to bed dead late.
But I have to go at seven
Even though I'm nearly eight!

I wish I was our Sammy.
He draws rudey women
Without arms or legs or even heads
In the cubicle when he goes swimming.
But I'm not allowed to go to the baths.
Me Mam says I have to wait.
Cos I might get drowned, cos I'm only seven.
But I'm not, I'm nearly eight.

I wish I was our Sammy.
He robbed me toy car you know.
Now the wheels are missing and the top's broke off
And, and the bleeding thing won't go.
And he said when he took it it was just like that
But it wasn't it went dead straight.
But you can't say nothing when they think you're seven
And you're not, you're nearly eight!

I wish I was our Sammy.
You know what he sometimes does?
He wees straight through the letter box
Of the house next door to us.
I tried to do it one night
But I had to stand on a crate
Cos I couldn't reach the letter box;
But I will by the time I'm eight!

[*He sits, bored and petulant, shoots an imaginary* **Sammy**.]

Act 2, scene 2

Edward, *a boy the same age, appears. He is, at once, bright and forthcoming.*

Eddie: Hellow.

Mickey: [*Suspicious*] Hello.

Eddie: I've seen you before.

Mickey: Where?

Eddie: You were playing with some other boys near my house.

Mickey: Do you live up by the park?

Eddie: Yes. Are you going to come and play there again?

Mickey: No. I would. But I'm not allowed.

Eddie: Why?

Mickey: I don't know.

Eddie: Well, I'm not allowed to play down here actually.

Mickey: Give us a sweet.

Eddie: All right. [*He begins to pull out a large bag of sweets*]

Mickey: [*Shocked*] What?

Eddie: [*Offering the bag*] Here.

Mickey: [*Suspiciously taking one. Trying to work out the catch.* **Eddie** *beaming brightly at him.* **Mickey** *takes one and saves it*] Can I have another one? For our Sammy.

Eddie: Yes of course. Take as many as you want.

Mickey: [*Taking a handful*] Are you soft?

Eddie: I don't think so.

Mickey: Round here if you ask anyone for a sweet you have to ask about, about twenty four million times you know. And you know what?

Eddie: [*Sitting beside him*] What?

Mickey: They still don't bleeding give you one. Sometimes our Sammy does but you have to be dead careful if Sammy gives you a sweet.

Eddie: Why?

Mickey: Because if Sammy gives you a sweet he's usually weed on it first.

Eddie: [*Exploding with giggles*] Oh that sounds like super fun.

Mickey: It is if you're our Sammy.

Eddie: Do you want to come and play?

Mickey: I might do. But I'm not playing now because I'm pissed off.

Eddie: [*Awed*] Pissed off! You say smashing things don't you? Pissed off. Do you know any more words like that?

Mickey: Yeh. Yeh I know loads of words like that. You know like the 'F' word.

Eddie: [*Clueless*] Pardon?

Mickey: You know, the 'F' word. [**Eddie** *puzzled still,* **Mickey** *checking that no one is around before whispering in* **Eddie**'s *ear. The two of them immediately wriggling and giggling with glee*]

Eddie: What does it mean?

Mickey: I don't know. It sounds good though, doesn't it?

Eddie: Fantastic. When I get home I shall look it up in the dictionary.

Mickey: In the what?

Eddie: In the dictionary. Don't you know what a dictionary is?

Mickey: 'Course I do. It's a thingy isn't it?

Eddie: A book which tells you the meaning of words.

Mickey: Yeh. I know.

Eddie: Will you be my best friend?

Mickey: Yeh. Yeh if you want.

Eddie: And I shall be your best friend. What's your name?

Mickey: Michael Johnston. But everyone calls me Mickey. What's yours?

Eddie: Edward.

Mickey: And they call you Eddie?

Eddie: No!

Mickey: Well I will.

Eddie: Will you?

Mickey: Yeh. How old are you, Eddie?

Eddie: Seven.

Mickey: I'm older than you. I'm nearly eight.

Eddie: Well I'm nearly eight really.

Mickey: When's your birthday?

Eddie: December the twelfth.

Mickey: So is mine.

Eddie: Is it really?

Mickey: Hey, we were born on the same day. That means we can be blood brothers. Do you want to be my blood brother, Eddie?

Eddie: What do I have to do?

Mickey: It hurts you know. [**Mickey** *taking out his penknife, cuts his hand*] Now give us your hand. [*Does the same to* **Eddie** *and then clamps the hands together*] See this means that we're blood brothers and that we always have to stand by each other. Now, you have to say, after me: 'I will always defend my brother . . . '

Eddie: I will always defend my brother . . .

The Mother: [*Off*] Mickey . . . Mickey . . .

Eddie: Is that your mummy?

[**The Mother** *appearing*]

Mickey: Mam, this is my brother.

The Mother: [*Stunned*] What?

Mickey: My blood brother, Eddie.

The Mother: Eddie. Eddie who?

Eddie: Edward Lyons, Mrs Johnston.

[**The Mother** *stares at him*]

Mickey: Eddie's my best friend now, Mam. He lives up by the park but . . .

The Mother: Mickey, get in the house . . .

Mickey: What?

The Mother: [*Threatening*] Get in!

[*The bright and eager smile disappears from* **Eddie**'s *face*]

Mickey: But I've only . . .

The Mother: Get!

Mickey: [*Going, almost crying*] I haven't done nothing. I'll see you, Eddie.

Eddie: Erm. Erm have I done something, Mrs Johnston?

The Mother: Does your mother know you're down here? [**Eddie** *shaking his head*] What would she say if she knew?

Eddie: I . . . I think she'd be angry.

The Mother: So don't you think you'd better go home before she finds out?

Eddie: I suppose so.

The Mother: Go on then.

[*He turns to go and then stops*]

Eddie: Could I . . . would it be all right if I came to play with Mickey on another day? Or perhaps he could come and play at my house . . .

The Mother: Don't you ever come around here again. Ever.

Eddie: But . . .

The Mother: Ever! Now go on . . . beat it . . . go on, go home before the bogey man gets you.

[*She watches as he leaves and stands, staring after him*]

Act 2, scene 3

She watches as the scene forms in which we see **Eddie** *at home,
leafing through a dictionary.* **Mrs Lyons** *entering and kissing
him on the head.* **Eddie** *turning and smiling at her*

Eddie: Mum ... Mummy ...

[**The Mother** *turns and leaves*]

Eddie: Mum how do you spell 'bogey man'?

Mrs Lyons: [*Laughing*] Wherever did you hear such a word?

Eddie: I erm ... I'm trying to look it up ... what is a bogey
man?

Mrs Lyons: [*Laughing*] Edward ... there's no such thing.
It's erm, it's just an idea of something bad. It's a, a
superstition. The sort of thing a silly mother would say to
her children 'the bogey man will get you'.

Eddie: Will he get me?

Mrs Lyons: Edward ... I've told you, there's no such thing.

[*There is a loud knocking at the door.* **Mrs Lyons** *goes off to
answer the door*]

Mickey: [*Off*] Does Eddie live here?

Mrs Lyons: Pardon?

Mickey: Does he? Is he coming out to play?

Eddie: [*Looking up. Delighted*] Mickey!

[**Mrs Lyons** *and* **Mickey** *entering*]

Mickey: Hiya, Eddie. Look, I've got our Sammy's catapult.
You coming out eh?

Eddie: [*Taking the catapult and trying a practice shot*] Ogh
... Isn't Mickey fantastic, Mum?

Mrs Lyons: Do you go to the same school as Edward?

Mickey: No.

Eddie: Mickey says smashing things. We're blood brothers, aren't we, Mickey?

Mickey: Yeh. We were born on the same day.

Eddie: Come on Mickey . . . Let's go . . .!

Mrs Lyons: Edward! Edward it's time for bed.

Eddie: Mummy, it's not.

Mrs Lyons: [*Ushering* **Mickey** *out*] I'm very sorry but it's Edward's bedtime.

Eddie: Mummy! Mummy, it's early! [**Mrs Lyons** *returning after having shown* **Mickey** *the door*] Mummy!

Mrs Lyons: Edward. Where did you meet that boy?

Eddie: [*Petulant*] At his house.

Mrs Lyons: His second name . . . his second name is Johnston . . . isn't it Edward?

Eddie: Yes! And I think you're very mean!

Mrs Lyons: I've told you never to go where that boy lives.

Eddie: But why?

Mrs Lyons: Because . . . because you're not the same as him. You're not! Do you understand?

Eddie: No! No I don't understand . . . And I hate you!

[*Instinctively she whacks him across the head but is immediately appalled*]

Mrs Lyons: Edward, Edward . . . [*Pulling him to her, cradling him*] Edward you must understand, it's for your own good. It's only because I love you, Edward.

Eddie: [*Breaking away. Complete rage*] You don't! If you loved me you'd let me go out with Mickey because he's my best friend. I like him more than you.

Mrs Lyons: Edward! Edward, don't say that.

Eddie: Well. Well it's true. I know what you are!

Mrs Lyons: What?

Eddie: You're a . . . you're a fuckoff!

[**Mrs Lyons** *lunges across the room, grabs him by the wrist and shakes the terrified child, screaming at him*]

Mrs Lyons: You see . . . you see why I don't want you mixing with boys like that. Filth; you learn filfth and you behave like this . . . like a horrible little boy . . . like them, like them . . . you're behaving like them and I won't have it, do you understand? [*She is slightly out of control, shaking him. He stares in terror*] You're my son, mine . . . you won't behave like them, like him . . . you won't . . . you won't . . . [*She suddenly sees the fear in his face. Almost crying she gently pulls him to her and cradles him*] Oh my son . . . my son . . .

[*The scene freezes*]

Act 2, scene 4

We see **Mickey** *and* **Linda***, a girl the same age, appear. They stand, craning until they spot* **Eddie***.*

Mickey: [*Loud conspiratorial whisper*] Eddie . . . Eddie . . . [**Eddie** *looking up*] You coming out?

Eddie: [*Equally loud whisper*] I . . . my mum says I haven't got to play with you.

Mickey: Well my mum says I haven't got to play with you. Don't take any notice of mothers. They're soft. Are you coming? I've got Linda with me. She's a girl. But she's all right. Come on, bunk under the fence and she won't see you.

[**Eddie** *looks from his mother to the two kids. Eventually decides to risk it. He creeps away. As he joins the others* **Mrs Lyons** *exits*]

Mickey: Hiya.

Eddie: Hiya, Mickey. Hello, Linda.

Linda: Hiya, Eddie. [*Producing an air pistol*] Look. We've got Sammy's air gun. Do you want to have a go?

Eddie: Yes, please.

Mickey: Come on, Eddie, you can come and have a shot at our target in the park.

Eddie: Which target?

Linda: Peter Pan.

Mickey: We always shoot at that don't we, Linda?

Linda: Yeh. You know what, Eddie, the last time we was there we nearly shot his thingy off.

Eddie: What, what's a thingy?

Linda: You know. [**Eddie** *is still puzzled*] Come here, I'll whisper it to you. [*She does so and the three of them break up with the giggles*]

Eddie: Agh.

Mickey: Come on gang . . . let's go . . . [*With an Indian call and arm wave he prepares to lead his men out*]

Eddie: [*Standing firm*] But, Mickey . . . I mean . . . are we allowed to do that?

Linda: What?

Eddie: Suppose we get caught. By a policeman.

Mickey: Agh . . . take no notice. We've been caught loads of times by a policeman. Haven't we, Linda?

Linda: Oh my God, yeh. Hundreds of times. More than that.

Mickey: We say dead funny things to them don't we, Linda.

Eddie: What sort of funny things?

Linda: All sorts don't we, Mickey. My God, yeh.

Mickey: You know like when they ask you what your name is, eh eh. Well we say, Linda, don't we, we say things like, like Adolf Hitler.

[**Eddie** *impressed and laughing with them*]

Linda: And tell him that other one Mickey, that we say to them . . .

Mickey: Yeh. Listen . . . listen; you know when a policeman says 'What do you think you're doing? – because they always say that – we say, don't we Linda, we say 'waiting for the ninety-two bus'.

Eddie: [*Greatly impressed as they exit*] Do you? Do you really?

Linda: Yeh. We're never frightened are we, Mickey?

Eddie: Goodness that's fantastic . . .

[*As kids run off* **The Mother** *enters as ghost. She sets the table, raises the shoes above her head and polishes the table*]

Act 2, scene 5

Mrs Lyons: [*Entering with telephone*] I want you to come home Richard . . . For God's sake leave the office . . . Because I don't know where Edward is . . . But out playing where? . . . There's nothing wrong with my nerves . . . It's, it's this place; I hate it, I want to move. It doesn't have to be far away . . . It's these people, these people Edward has begun mixing with . . . You don't see it Richard. You don't see how he's drawn to them . . . I don't need to see the doctor. [*Making an effort to control herself*] I'm fine. I'm fine. I just want to move away from this neighbourhood . . . Well I'm frightened. I'm frightened for Edward. Please . . . please . . . pl . . . [*He has hung up. She replaces the receiver.*

As she does so, **The Mother** *looks up and slowly places the shoes on the table.* **Mrs Lyons** *screams and runs off*

Act 2, scene 6

The children run on with the airpistol. **Mickey** *takes aim. He fires.*

Linda: Missed!

[**Eddie** *loads and fires*]

Linda: Missed!

[*She loads and fires. There is a clunk as she hits.* **Mickey** *loads and fires*]

Linda: Missed!

[**Eddie** *loads and fires*]

Linda: Missed!

[*She loads and fires. There is a clunk as she hits*]

Mickey: [*Takes gun*] We're not playing with the gun no more.

Linda: Ah why?

Mickey: It gets broke if you use it too much.

Eddie: What are we going to do now, Mickey?

Linda: Go on tell us, tell us.

Mickey: I'll tell ya.

Linda: What?

Mickey: We're going to throw some stones through those windows there.

Linda: I'm going for me tea now.

Mickey: Scared.

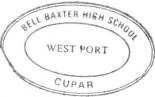

BELL BAXTER HIGH SCHOOL

WEST PORT

CUPAR

Linda: I'm not. We're having chips. I'm going. [*Exits*]

Mickey: You're not scared are you, Eddie?

Eddie: No.

Mickey: Here's your stone. You've got to throw in through that window there, right? After three. One, two, three ...

Policewoman: [*entering*] ... Me mother caught a flea. She put it in the teapot to make a pot of tea ...
... And what do you think you're doing?

Eddie: [*Very excited*] Adolf Hitler!

Policewoman: What's your name, son?

Eddie: Waiting for a ninety-two bus ...

Mickey: He's not with me ...

[*The Mothers enter*]

Act 2, scene 7

Policewoman: [*To* **Mrs Johnston**] And he was about to commit a serious crime, love, a serious crime. Now do you understand that? [**The Mother** *nods*] You don't want to end up in court again, do you? Eh? [*Shakes her head*] Because that's what's going to happen if I have any more trouble from one of yours. I warned you last time didn't I, Mrs Johnston, over your Sammy, didn't I? [*She nods*] Well there'll be no more warnings from now on. You keep them in order or it'll be the courts for you, or worse. Won't it? [*She nods*] Yes, it will.

[**The Mother** *and* **Mickey** *exit.* **Policewoman** *turns and approaches* **Mrs Lyons**]

As I say, it was more of a prank really, Mrs Lyons. I'd just dock his pocket money if I was you. But one thing I would say, and excuse me if I'm interfering, but I'd not let him mix with the likes of them in future. Make sure he keeps with his own kind, Mrs Lyons, not running round with them at the other end. Well, er thanks for the drink. All the best now. Tarar. [*She leaves*]

Mrs Lyons: Edward. Edward, how would you like to move to another house?

Eddie: Why, Mummy?

Mrs Lyons: Erm, well, various reasons really; but, erm, well Mummy's not too well and we thought we'd move a bit further out, towards the country somewhere. Do you think you'd like that? [*Exits*]

Eddie: I want to stay here.

Act 2, scene 8

The Mother: [*Enters and stands as if in office*] [*To audience*] You see, and I just feel that if I could leave here and, and, you know, sort of start again, in a new house, in a new place where I wasn't known, where the kids weren't known, well we could start again with a clean sheet. Do you know what I mean? You know if we could just like, find a place to start again. See, we've tried, here. We've tried to like turn over to a new page, but like, like the blotches keep showing through. But if we could move. [*Pause*] Well could you put me on the waiting list? Please. Thank you. [*Pause*] Well even if it is a few years, I mean as long as I knew there was a chance well, well it'd be something to hold on to, wouldn't it?

Eddie: Hello, Mrs Johnston. How are you? [*She looks at him and suddenly her face breaks into a smile and she laughs*] I'm sorry. Is there something wrong?

The Mother: No! I just don't usually have kids enquiring about my health. I er, I'm all right. And how are you, Master Lyons?

Eddie: Very well, thank you, Mrs Johnston.

[*She looks at him for a moment*]

The Mother: Yeh. You look it. You look very well. Does your mother look after you?

Eddie: Of course.

The Mother: Listen, I told you not to come to our house again.

Eddie: I'm sorry, but I just wanted to see Mickey.

The Mother: No. It's best . . . if . . .

Eddie: I won't be coming here again. Ever. We're moving away, to the country.

The Mother: Lucky you.

Eddie: But I'd much rather live here.

The Mother: Would you? When are you going?

Eddie: Tomorrow.

The Mother: So we won't see you again, eh? [**Eddie** *shakes his head and quietly begins to cry*] What's up?

Eddie: [*Through the tears*] I don't want to go. I want to stay here, where my friends are, where Mickey is.

The Mother: Come here. [*She takes him, cradles him to her, letting him cry*] Now listen, listen . . . don't be silly. You'll probably love it in your new house. You'll meet lots of new friends. In no time at all you'll forget Mickey ever existed.

Eddie: I won't. I won't, I'll never forget.

The Mother: Shush . . . shush . . . Listen, listen, Eddie; here's you wanting to stay, and here's me, I've been trying to get out for years. We're a right pair, aren't we?

Eddie: Why don't you, Mrs Johnston? Why don't you buy a new house near us?

The Mother: Just like that?

Eddie: Yes, yes!

[**The Mother** *looks at him and laughs*]

The Mother: Mickey's round the back. Go on, you can go and see him. But don't blame me if your mother finds out.

Eddie: Thank you. Thank you, Mrs Johnston. [*He looks at her for a moment too long*]

The Mother: What you looking at?

Eddie: I thought you didn't like me. I thought you weren't very nice. But I think you're smashing.

The Mother: [*Looking at him*] God help the girls when you start dancing.

Eddie: Pardon?

The Mother: Nothing. Now go on. Beat it. Go and see our Mickey before I change me mind.

Eddie: Goodbye, Mrs Johnston. [**Mrs Lyons** *enters in outdoor clothes*] Goodbye.

Act 2, scene 9

Birdsong. **The Mother** *watches them for a moment before she exits.*

Mrs Lyons: Well Edward, do you like it here?

Eddie: [*Unenthusiastic*] It's very nice.

Mrs Lyons: [*Bending and pointing*] Look Edward . . . look at those cows . . . and those trees. Oh Edward, you're going to like it so much out here, aren't you?

Eddie: Yes. Are you feeling better now, Mummy?

Mrs Lyons: Much better darling. Oh look, Edward . . . look, look at those birds . . . look at that lovely black and white one . . .

Eddie: [*Immediately covering his eyes*] Don't Mummy, don't . . . don't look . . .

Mrs Lyons: Edward!

Eddie: It's a magpie. Never look at one magpie. It's one for sorrow.

Mrs Lyons: Edward, that's just a silly superstition.

Eddie: It's not, it's not, Mickey told . . . me . . .

Mrs Lyons: Edward, I think we can forget the silly things that Mickey says.

Eddie: I'm going inside, I want to read.

Mrs Lyons: Edward, children take time to adapt to new surroundings. But you soon won't even remember that you once lived somewhere else. In a few weeks you'll forget him – Mickey. [*She smiles at him and nods. They stand together for a moment, surveying the land before them*]

Eddie: What's that Mummy?

Mrs Lyons: [*Craning to see*] What?

Eddie: There . . . look . . . below the hill

Mrs Lyons: What? Oh those houses? That's the beginning of a council estate. But we've arranged with the gardener, he's going to plant a row of poplars down at the end of the paddock there. Once they're in we won't even be able to see that estate. Oh, I love it out here. I feel secure here. I feel warm and safe. Once the trees are planted we won't even see that estate. [*She beams a smile at him as they turn and head for the house*]

Act 2, scene 10

As they exit we see **Mickey** *and* **The Mother** *enter, each carrying a suitcase.* **The Mother** *is vigorously taking in the fresh air and leading the way as* **Mickey** *struggles with the case, behind her. He is now twelve.*

Mickey: [*Stopping and pointing*] Is that our new house there Mam?

The Mother: [*Looking*] Where?

Mickey: There . . . look, you can just see it behind that row of trees.

The Mother: [*Laughing*] Mickey . . . give over will you. The Corporation don't build houses like that. That's a private house son. [*She points in the other direction*] No . . . look, down the hill . . . that's where ours is. Look. Oh . . . son, isn't it nice out here eh? Eh?

Mickey: It's like the country isn't it, Mam?

The Mother: Eh, we'll be all right here, son. Away from the muck and the dirt. And the bloody trouble. You can breathe out here, Mickey. Hey, I could dance. Couldn't you?

Mickey: [*Alarmed*] What?

The Mother: [*Grabbing him*] Come on . . . [*She lilts the tune and waltzes him around the road as he protests vigorously*]

Mickey: Mother . . . Mother put me down will you. [*Breaking away, leaving his mother to dance alone, looking around and checking that nobody saw him then watching his mother as she dances. Slowly a huge smile breaking across his face*]

The Mother: And what are you laughing at? I used to be a good dancer you know. A very good dancer in fact.

Mickey: I'm not laughing. I'm smiling. I haven't seen you happy like this for ages.

The Mother: Well I'm happy now. You never know, Mickey, play your cards right, we might have tea from the chippie.

Mickey: [*Picking up his case as does* **The Mother**] Ooh, can we, Mam, can we?

The Mother: Come on, come on. Hey, Jesus, where's the others? Where's our Sammy and the others?

Mickey: They went into that field, Mam.

The Mother: Which field?

Mickey: [*Pointing*] That field.

The Mother: [*Craning. Horror stricken. Shouting*] Sammy, Sammy get off that cow before I bleedin kill you. Oh Jeez, what's our Donna Marie put her sodding foot in? Sammy, get hold of her . . . wipe it off . . . oh . . . come on, Mickey . . . come on . . .

[*Exit*]

Act 2, scene 11

Mrs Lyons *enters. She is terrified.*

Narrator:
There's no use clutching at your rosary
The Devil's in the garden and he can see
Deep inside; he can touch your bones.
No he won't, no he's never going to let you alone.
You can run you can hide but he'll always find you
Wherever you are he's just behind you.
When he rings at the chimes then he knows you're in
No you won't, no you'll never get away from him,
No you won't, no you'll never get away from him.

[*Repeats last line. Ends with scream from* **Mrs Lyons**]

Eddie: [*Enters as* **Narrator** *exits*] Mummy, Mummy, what's wrong?

Mrs Lyons: She's following . . .

Eddie: Who Mummy?

Mrs Lyons: Wherever I go she will follow. Follow . . .

Eddie: Shall I tell Daddy to telephone for the doctor?

Mrs Lyons: No. I don't need to see the doctor. Edward, you will have to go away to school.

Eddie: But I'm perfectly happy here. [*He reaches out to her*]

Mrs Lyons: [*Seizing his hand*] Edward . . . I love you terribly, you know.

[*They exit together*]

Act 3, scene 1

[*Two years later*]

Mickey *enters with box to sit on.*

Linda: [*Enters. They are both now fourteen*] Tch . . . Oh hey, Mickey. I've got mud all over me shoes. You didn't say it was across a load of fields.

Mickey: Stop moaning, Linda. You were the one who wanted to come up here with me.

Linda: I didn't. You said; you said forget school and come with you.

Mickey: Look. [*Points*] You can see the estate from up here.

Linda: You what? You mean we've come all the way up here just to look at the estate?

Mickey: Erm . . . well I thought . . . er . . .

Linda: Do you want to come and sit by me?

Mickey: [*Swallowing*] What? Yeh. If you want.

Linda: Tch.

[*He goes and sits by her*]

Mickey: Do you er . . .?

Linda: [*Eager*] What?

Mickey: Do you erm . . . What do you want to do?

Linda: I don't know. What would you suggest, Mickey?

Mickey: [*Panic stricken*] What?

Linda: What would you like to do, Mickey?

Mickey: Erm . . . or . . . maybe . . . maybe we should have brought our Sammy's air gun.

Linda: What the hell do we want an air gun for?

Mickey: I thought you liked firing the air gun.

Linda: Mickey. I'm fourteen now. So are you! Don't you think we're a bit old for air guns, and catapults?

Mickey: Yeh. Yeh I suppose we are.

Linda: I mean, can't you think of anything else me and you could do?

Mickey: Course I can.

Linda: What, Mickey? What?

Mickey: [*Staring at her*] Erm [*Bottling out*] We could go robbing apples.

Linda: Oh . . .

Mickey: [*Fast*] There's an orchard in that big house, do you want me to go and rob some?

Linda: No. I don't. And anyway. You'd get caught. I saw someone in the garden.

Mickey: That lad. I see him sometimes when I'm up here.

Linda: He's very good looking.

Mickey: What?

Linda: You could tell, even from far away that he's very good looking.

Mickey: [*Rattled*] All right, all right, you've told me once.

Linda: Oh I'm very sorry. I'm going back to school.

Mickey: I thought you were staying with me.

Linda: I was. But I didn't know you'd still be wanting to go robbing apples and play with air guns.

Mickey: I don't.

Linda: Well what do you want to do?

Mickey: Well, well . . . well what do you want to do, Linda?

Linda: Tch. I'm going. [*She does so.* **Mickey** *watches her going. When she is far enough not to hear he shouts*]

Mickey: I'll tell you what I want to do, Linda. I want to kiss you and put me arms around you and kiss you and kiss you. But I just don't know how to tell you, because I've got pimples, me feet are too big and me bum sticks out and and . . . agh . . . [*He stands watching her, wistful and absorbed. He doesn't see* **Eddie** *appear behind him*]

Act 3, scene 2

Eddie: Hello.

Mickey: [*Turning*] Hello. Eddie.

Eddie: How do you know . . .

Mickey: [*Laughing*] Don't you recognize me?

Eddie: I have seen you up here before but . . .

Mickey: 'A blood brother should always recognize his brother, defend his brother, support . . .'

Eddie: Mickey?

Mickey: [*Laughing*] Yeh . . .

Eddie: My God do you . . .

Mickey: Yeh, I live down there.

Eddie: I live just . . .

Mickey: I know . . .

Eddie: Well sodding hell. [**Mickey** *laughing*] What's wrong?

Mickey: You. It sounds dead funny swearing in a posh voice.

Eddie: Which posh voice?

Mickey: That one.

Eddie: That girl I saw you with was that . . .

Mickey: Linda, yeh.

Eddie: Is she erm, is she your girlfriend?

Mickey: Yeh. Yeh. We've been erm, yeh, going out together for ages now.

Eddie: [*Awed*] Really? And do you erm, you know, do you . . .

Mickey: What?

Eddie: You know, kiss and that?

Mickey: All the time. See, me and Linda . . . we're in love.

Eddie: Are you?

Mickey: Yeh. [*Pause*] Have you got a girlfriend?

Eddie: Me? Oh, yes, of course.

Mickey: [*Impressed*] Have you?

Eddie: Mm.

Mickey: And do you ... you know?

Eddie: Oh yes, all the time. Would you like to see her picture?

Mickey: What?

[**Eddie** *producing a wallet and taking out a picture. He gives* **Mickey** *a cursory glance at it*]

Mickey: Come here ... let's have a proper look ... [**Mickey** *takes the picture*] Her?

Eddie: Yes. Her name is Yvette.

Mickey: [*Looking from the picture to* **Eddie**] Haven't I seen her on the telly?

Eddie: No, no, she does look like somebody on the television.

Mickey: Oh. [*Pause*] That didn't look like a real photo, Eddie.

Eddie: Pardon?

Mickey: It looked like a picture you'd cut out of a magazine.

Eddie: Well it is, from a magazine. She isn't really my girlfriend. I haven't got a girlfriend.

Mickey: [*Laughing*] Neither have I.

Eddie: But Linda, you said ...

Mickey: I know but she's not. See, I mean I know she would be. She would go out with me, I know that but it's just ...

Eddie: What?

Mickey: It's just dead difficult.

Eddie: Talking to girls? [**Mickey** *nodding*] Yes I know ... but you must, Mickey ... you must.

Mickey: I know that. Every time I see her I promise meself I'll ask her but, but the words just disappear.

Eddie: But you mustn't let them.

Mickey: What do I say though?

Eddie: Look, I'll tell you what to say. Next time you see Linda you stare straight into her eyes, bold and unflinching and in a steady firm voice you say: 'Linda, my loins are burning for you. [**Mickey** *screaming with laughter*] Let me lay my weary head upon your warm breast; Linda, I love you, I want you, the very centre of my being calls out for you! And then, and then Mickey, her eyes will be heavy lidded and half closed and her voice will be husky and desperate as she says, as she moans 'Oh Mickey, take me, take me'.

[**Mickey** *screams with laughter. The laughter eventually subsides.* **Mickey** *stares straight ahead, thinking*]

Eddie: It would work, you know!

Mickey: You're a case you are, Eddie, a case. Do you know something, I'm really glad I met you again.

[**Eddie** *looks up, laughs*]

Eddie: Here [*Holds out his blood brother hand*] Do you remember?

[**Mickey** *clasps his hand. From off we hear* **Mrs Lyons** *calling* 'Edward . . . Edward']

Mickey: Is that your old girl?

Eddie: Yes.

Mickey: I'd better be off.

Eddie: Why?

Mickey: She used to hate me.

Eddie: I don't think she meant you any harm, Mickey. The thing is, she's ill. She was probably ill even then.

Mickey: What's wrong with her?

Eddie: It's a sort of paranoia.

Mickey: What?

Eddie: Mental illness.

Mrs Lyons: [*Entering*] Edward. Edward are you still here?

Mickey: [*Looking at her*] Yeh, well I'd better ... Erm. Listen, Eddie, we hang out by the chippie most nights. Why don't you come down some time?

Eddie: OK. Perhaps when I'm next home from school. It's only Mickey, Mum. You remember Mickey, don't you?

Mrs Lyons: Yes. He's following me, isn't he?

Eddie: Mum, he's just ...

Mrs Lyons: And so is she. She's put a curse upon me you know, Edward. She's waiting to kill you.

Mickey: Jesus Christ.

Eddie: [*Laughing at* **Mickey**'s *alarm*] It's all right. This is normal.

Mickey: I'll er ... I'll see you, Eddie.

[*As he exits* **Eddie** *takes his mother and leads her back inside*]

Mrs Lyons: She's trying to make me tell you, Edward. But I won't. I shan't kill you, Edward.

Eddie: Good. Good.

[**Mickey** *watches them go*]

Act 4, scene 1

[*Three years later*]

Linda: [*Off calling, bright*]

Mickey: Linda. Linda . . . Eddie . . .

[**Narrator** *enters*]

Narrator:
> There's a jingle in your pocket, and you've got good friends
> And it seems that the summer's never ever going to end.
> When you're sweet sixteen and you haven't got a care
> Apart from deciding on the clothes you're going to wear.
> You can stand outside for hours, just talking through the night
> Or until Mrs Wong switches off the chippy light.
> The movies are all magic and the radio's singing dreams
> The days go on forever for the sweet seventeens.
> The Devil's hardly visible, he took a holiday
> The Bogey Man, it seems, packed his bags and moved away.
> The streets are technicoloured like a movie scene
> The days are free and endless when you're nearly eighteen
> Yes the days are free and endless when you're nearly eighteen.

[*Throughout the above we see* **Mickey**, **Eddie** *and* **Linda** *in what should be snapshot images, the three of them at the pictures, the three of them, arms around each other smiling for a camera, the three of them eating chips, the three of them in a car.* **Eddie** *and* **Linda** *looning,* **Mickey** *watching and* *laughing.* **Mickey** *and* **Linda** *looning around,* **Eddie** *watching.* **Mickey** *and* **Eddie** *camping it up,* **Linda** *laughing. As the* **Narrator** *closes we see* **Eddie***, dancing with* **Linda***, ostentatiously waltzing her.* **Mickey** *exits*]

Linda: Eddie ... Eddie ... get off [*Laughing*] For God's sake, you're making a show of me ... Eddie ...

Eddie: For you, sweet Linda, I would suffer a thousand things more than embarrassment. [*And he makes a great show of sinking to one knee*]

Linda: [*Anxious not to be seen with this loony*] Tch ... Eddie, get up. You're a nutter.

Eddie: It's been a terrific summer hasn't it?

Linda: It's been great.

Eddie: I love it when we're together, you know, the three of us.

Linda: So do I.

Eddie: But we can't be any longer!

Linda: Why?

Eddie: I ... I go away to university tomorrow.

Linda: Tomorrow? You didn't tell us.

Eddie: I know. I think I've been pretending that if I didn't mention it the day wouldn't come around. Can I write to you?

Linda: If you want.

Eddie: Would Mickey mind?

Linda: Mickey, why should he?

Eddie: Because you're his girlfriend.

Linda: I'm not.

Eddie: You are.

Linda: I'm not ... he hasn't asked me.

Eddie: [*Laughing*] You mean he still hasn't?

Linda: [*Laughing*] No.

Eddie: But it's ridiculous.

Linda: I know, I hope for his sake he never has to ask me to marry him. It'll take him twenty years to get around to it.

Eddie: He's mad. If I was Mickey I would have asked you ages ago.

Linda: I know you would.

Eddie: If I was Mickey, if I was Mickey I'd have said: 'You are my girlfriend because I love you. And every moment I am away from you, you are in my thoughts. And even, even if I were never to see you again, there would not be a day in which I did not think of you.'

[**Linda** *smiles at him*]

Mickey: [*Off*] Linda . . . Eddie . . . [**Mickey** *enters*]

Eddie: Hiya, Mickey.

Linda: Where've you been, Mick? We've been waitin' for you.

Mickey: Agh . . . I had to do some bleeding overtime. I hate that place.

Eddie: Mickey, I'm going away tomorrow . . . to university.

Mickey: What? You didn't say.

Eddie: I know. Now the thing is I won't be back until Christmas. Three months. Now you don't want me to continue in suspense for another three months do you?

Mickey: What?

Linda: What are you on about?

Eddie: Will you talk to Linda, Mickey? I'd like to know the outcome.

Mickey: What?

Linda: Eddie! Tch.

Eddie: Go on. Go on.

[**Mickey** *turns and goes to* **Linda**]

Mickey: Erm . . . Linda . . .

Linda: What Mickey?

Mickey: Erm . . . er, well the thing is the centre of my . . . being cries out for . . . erm, my knees, loins are . . . [*Snaps*] Linda, for Christ's sake will you go out with me?

Linda: [*Just as fast*] Yeh.

Mickey: [*Pause*] Erm . . . good. Well I suppose I better . . . well er . . . Come here. [*He grabs her quickly, embraces and kisses her*]

Linda: [*Fighting for air*] My God. You take your time getting off the starting block, but when you do there's no stopping you.

Mickey: [*Delighted*] I know . . . give us another kiss. [*They kiss again*]

[*We see* **Eddie***, apart from it. At first watching but then turning away. He begins to wander away*]

Mickey: Eddie . . . Eddie, where are you going? I thought we were going to the club, there's a dance.

Eddie: No, I've got to er . . . I've got to pack for tomorrow.

Mickey: Are you sure? [**Eddie** *nodding*] See you at Christmas then, eh Eddie. Listen, I'm going to do a load of overtime between now and Christmas, the Christmas party'll be on me. Eh?

Eddie: Right. It's a deal. See you.

Linda: [*Pushes quickly across and kisses him lightly on the face*] Thanks Eddie

Mickey: Yeh. Thanks Eddie. [*They go their separate ways*]

Act 4, scene 2

Narrator:

It was one day in October when the sun began to rain

It seems the Devil hadn't left he'd only found a different name;

They were calling him Inflation, and Recession was his Son.

And all bowed down before them as their work was done.

Yes, all bowed down before them as their deeds were done.

[*From the rest of the company a few bars of 'Ding dong merrily on high' as* **Eddie** *enters in duffle coat and college scarf. Unseen by* **Mickey,** **Eddie** *creeps up behind him and puts his hands over* **Mickey's** *eyes. Carol stops*]

Eddie: Guess who?

Mickey: Father Christmas!

Eddie: [*Leaping in front of* **Mickey**] Mickey . . . [*Laughing*] Merry Christmas. [**Mickey** *looking at him, unamused, and then looking away*] Come on then . . . I'm back. Where's the action, the booze, the Christmas parties, the music and the birds? [*Still no reaction from* **Mickey**] What's wrong, Mickey?

Mickey: Nothing. How's university?

Eddie: Fantastic. I haven't been to so many parties in my life. Oh, there's just so many tremendous people there, Mickey. But you'll meet them, some of them – Baz, Ronnie and Clare and, oh lots of them. They're coming over to stay for the New Year. For the party. Oh it's just, it's great Mickey.

Mickey: Good.

Eddie: [*Pause*] Come on. What's wrong with you? It's nearly Christmas. We were going to do everything. How's Linda?

Mickey: OK.

Eddie: [*Trying once more to rally him*] Well come on, let's go then . . . come on . . .

Mickey: Come on where?

Eddie: Mickey, what's wrong?

Mickey: [*Slowly looking up and at him*] You. You're a dick head. [**Eddie** *slightly unsure but laughing anyway*] There are no parties arranged. There is no booze or music. Christmas? I've had enough of Christmas and it isn't even here yet. See, there's very little to celebrate Eddie. Since you left I've been walking round all day, every day, looking for a job.

Eddie: What about the job you had?

Mickey: It disappeared. [*Pause*] You know something, I was dead glad at first; because I bleeding hated it, standing there all day never doing anything apart from putting cardboard boxes together. I used to get terrified that I'd have to do it for the rest of me life. So when they give me the knockback I was glad. But after three months of nothing, the same answer, nothing, nothing down for you – I'd crawl back to that job for half the money and double the hours. Just making up boxes it was. But after being fucked off from everywhere it seems like it was paradise.

Eddie: [*Pause, looking at him*] Why is, why is a job so important? If I couldn't get a job I'd just say 'sod it' and draw the dole, live like a bohemian, tilt my hat to the world and say 'screw you'. So, you're not working. Why is it so important?

Mickey: [*Looks at him*] You don't understand anything do you? I can't tilt me hat at the world, Eddie. I haven't got a hat. And if I did I'd look soft in it.

Eddie: Look, come on. I've got money, lots of it. I'm back, let's forget about bloody jobs, let's go and get Linda and celebrate. Look, look, money, lots of it, have some. [*Tries to thrust it into his hand*]

Mickey: NO! I don't want your money. Stuff it. [**Mickey** *watches as* **Eddie** *turns and picks up the notes.* **Eddie** *standing and looking at him*] Eddie, do me a favour will you? Piss off.

Eddie: [*Pause*] I thought . . . I thought we always stuck together. I thought we were . . . blood brothers.

Mickey: That was kids' stuff, Eddie, didn't anyone tell you? [*Pause.* **Mickey** *looking at him. An ironic snort*] But I suppose you still are a kid, aren't you?

Eddie: I'm exactly the same age as you.

Mickey: Yeh. But you're still a kid. I wish I could still be that as well, Eddie . . . and believe in all that blood brother stuff. But I can't. Because while no one was looking, I grew up. And you didn't. Because you didn't need to. I don't blame you for it Eddie. If I was in your shoes I'd be the same. But I'm in these shoes, looking at you. And you make me sick! Right? That was all just kids' stuff, Eddie, and I don't want to be reminded of it. Right? So just, just take yourself away. Go and see your friends and celebrate with them. [*Pause*] Go on . . . beat it before I hit you.

[**Eddie** *looks and then slowly backs away*]

Act 4, scene 3

Linda *enters*

Eddie: Linda . . . Linda . . . [*Reluctantly she stops*] Hello

Linda.

Linda: Hello Eddie.

Eddie: I've ... I've been home three weeks.

Linda: Oh.

Eddie: Why haven't you called to see me?

Linda: [*Shrugs*] I heard you had friends ... I, I didn't want to butt in.

Eddie: Linda. You'd never be butting in. I wouldn't care if I never saw those friends again, if I could be with you.

Linda: Eddie!

Eddie: What? If I'm never going to see you again I might as well tell you; you must have known anyway. I've always loved you. I'm sorry.

Linda: It's all right. Thanks for saying it. I'll remember. [*Looks at him*] I suppose ... I suppose I always felt the same. I always loved you as much as Mickey.

Eddie: Then marry me. [**Linda** *looks, and then laughs*] I mean it, and don't say I'm a kid, because I'm not.

Linda: I thought Mickey had told you. We got married two weeks before you came home. I'm having a baby.

Eddie: [*Reeling .. eventually*] Why didn't you let me know?

Linda: We tried. We went up to your house to get the address of your university. We wanted to invite you. But your mother just screamed at us. Something about Mickey following her. See you Eddie. [*Pause*] You'd better get a move on; your party will have started. [*She begins to go. Turns*] Happy New Year, Eddie.

Eddie: Linda! [*She stops. He crosses to her. Hands her a slip of paper*] I, erm, if Mickey takes this to my father's factory on Monday he'll be fixed up with a job. He needn't know it was anything to do with me. [*He quickly turns and goes*]

Act 5, scene 1

[*Some years later,* **Mr Lyons**' *factory*]

We see **Mickey** *enter and take his place on a production line*

Linda *as* **Narrator:**
So now you're clocking in, you're standing on the line
Doing two split shifts and all the overtime.
Till it gets that you never know the night from the day
But you're grateful, you're working, you're earning your pay.
And you do it for the kids; giving them a better life
Though you hardly ever see them, it's the same with the wife.
She wants to go out dancing but you've forgotten how.
Dancing's just for youngsters, you're an old man now.
Three cheers for the workhouse donkey who's old before his time.
He only has what's given, he's always on the line.

[**Eddie**, *now a bright young executive, walks past on the factory floor.* **Mickey** *doesn't notice him.* **Eddie** *stops and goes back a few paces*]

Eddie: Erm . . . it's . . . is it Mickey?

Mickey: [*Staring*] Hello.

Eddie: Hello, Mickey.

Mickey: Hello.

Eddie: I didn't recognize you for a moment. You look a lot, a lot older.

Mickey: Yeh. Yeh I suppose so. You er, you work here?

Eddie: Yes. I . . . when my father died I took his place on the board. How are you, Mickey, how's Linda and . . .

Mickey: All right. Look I'll ... [*Trying to get back to his work*]

Eddie: Look, why don't we have a drink together some time? Mm? [**Mickey**, *looking around him, nervously*] What's wrong?

Mickey: Look it's ... It's the other lads ... they're looking.

Eddie: Pardon?

Mickey: You, standing here, talking to me. You're a boss. It, you see, we're not supposed to ...

Eddie: For God's sake. We can have a conversation, can't we? I mean we both work in the same place, don't we? Don't we?

Mickey: Yeh. Yeh we both work in the same place. But you own the place, Mr Lyons.

Eddie: [*Pause*] Mickey ... the ... there are other jobs you could do here. Better jobs ... it could be arranged ... I could ...

Mickey: Listen! This job stinks. Right. Stinks! But it's my job. I got this job. An' it might be the worst bleeding job in the place but it's *mine*. I wasn't given it! Now if you don't mind I'll get on with it. Tarar. Mr Lyons.

[*They both exit*]

Act 5, scene 2

Linda *enters. Addresses audience as though it were official person at the housing department.*

Linda: See ... see we've been living with his mother for five years now ... Yeh, yeh I know that but we have applied ... But I thought we'd be moved by now ... we don't want a flat ... we want a house ... Well, well couldn't I see someone else ... couldn't I see who's in charge, the Chairman of the housing? I know he's a very busy man ... but what do you think I am? Don't you think I'm busy? Don't you think I get sick to the teeth of standing on the other side of a desk talking to people who never sodding well listen? Well I want to see the Chairman of the housing committee and until I do I'm not moving from this office ... [*She determinedly sits on the floor and prepares for a long wait*]

Eddie: [*Entering from office, carrying sheaf of papers*] Now look I'm afraid this won't get us anywhere; you've got to realize madam that ... Linda!

Linda: Oh. Are you? The Chairman?

Eddie: [*Nodding, laughing*] You look very funny sitting there you know. Don't you think you'd better come into my office? [*He offers his hand, she takes it, gets up and follows him*] Now what's the problem? [*They enter an 'office'.* **Eddie** *replacing telephone*] Now? Where's the problem? You can move in next week. [*Smiles*]

Linda: Eddie. Thanks! Eddie, we've been trying to get moved for five years. You fix it up in five minutes!

Eddie: Exactly. You should have asked me earlier.

Linda: I didn't even know you were living round here. Mickey never said he'd met you.

Eddie: No. He feels ... I don't think, by the way, that you'd better mention this to Mickey.

Linda: Eddie, I don't know what we'd do without you.

Eddie: It's nothing. What's a phone call? Please stop thanking me.

Linda: All right. Thanks. [*Laughs*] There I go again. Well, I better go. The kids'll be home from school and ... it's been smashing talking to you Eddie.

Eddie: Then ... then why don't we do it again?

Linda: Pardon?

Eddie: Talk. Meet. For lunch, perhaps.

Linda: Oh no Eddie ... I don't think ...

Eddie: Linda ... I'm not suggesting anything more. I know that you're married, to Mickey. And I'm not suggesting ... But would there be any harm in us occasionally meeting? Talking. Come to lunch next week.

Linda: Eddie ... I don't know ... I mean ...

Eddie: [*Light*] Oh for God's sake Linda, where's your sense of adventure gone? Go on, say yes ... you might enjoy yourself.

Linda: [*Pause*] Yeh ... yeh that's what I'm afraid of Eddie!

[**Eddie** *exits.* **Linda** *turns, to mirror. Begins to get her make up and hair together*]

The Mother *as* **Narrator:**

There's a girl inside the woman who's waiting to get free.

She's washed a million dishes and she's always making tea.

They think she's just a mother with nothing left inside

Who swapped her dreams for drudgery the day she was a bride.

But her dreams were not forgotten, just wrapped and packed away

In the hope that she could take them out and dust them off one day

There's a half remembered song comes to her lips again

There's a girl inside the woman and the mother she became.

[**Mickey** *enters and grabs her, threatening*]

Mickey: Just don't lie, Linda ... don't lie! Right. Our Sammy saw you with him. Sammy saw you.

Linda: [*Breaking free*] All right, all right so Sammy saw me with Eddie. What did he see? He saw me coming out of a restaurant with him for God's sake. That's not an affair. I've told you Mickey, I've just been out with him a few times.

Mickey: I could kill you! Why? Why did you go out with him?

Linda: Why? Why do you bloody well think? To get out of this place. To talk to someone apart from the kids ... to just, just be treated like someone who matters. When do I ever see you these days, Mickey?

Mickey: [*Shouting*] What am I supposed to do, stay home from work to talk to you?

Linda: [*Pause*] No. No. But what am I supposed to do? Just grow old?

Mickey: Why has he done this to me?

Linda: He hasn't done anything to you, Mickey, it's not like that ...

Mickey: The bastard. I'll get him!

Linda: [*Grabbing and restraining him*] Get him? Get him for what? Are you thick? Don't you realize, Mickey, he's just about the only friend you've got?

Mickey: Friend? Friend!

Linda: Friend. Yes. For Christ's sake, Mickey, how do you think you got your job? How do you think you escaped being one of those made redundant?

Mickey: What?

Linda: Eddie. Yes. Eddie arranged your job for you. Eddie made sure you weren't thrown out when the redundancies came. How do you think we got out of your mother's and into this house? Eddie arranged it. Eddie.

Mickey: Eddie. Eddie! [*Laughs, ironic*] And I thought it was mine. I thought it was my job. My house ... my wife ...

Linda: Don't be stupid. Eddie has a position. He can arrange these things and so he did.

Mickey: Have I got anything that doesn't belong to Eddie?

Linda: Mickey. I've told you we're just friends.

Mickey: Friends ... I'll give you friends! Yeh ... you were friends when you were first pregnant. Does my son belong to Eddie as well?

Linda: You bastard! [**Mickey** *turns and goes*] Mickey ... Mickey ... Where are you going?

Mickey: I'm going to get our Sammy. And we're going to pay a visit to your friend!

Linda: Mickey ... Mickey! [**Linda**, *frantic, eventually, picks up the phone*]

Act 5, scene 3

Mrs Lyons *enters with phone.*

Linda: Eddie ... can I please speak to Eddie.

Mrs Lyons: Eddie? Eddie who? I'm afraid there's no Eddie here.

Linda: Edward. Edward ... please let me speak to Edward.

Mrs Lyons: Oh no ... I couldn't do that; you're one of those who want to tell him.

Linda: Someone's coming after him, listen . . .

[*But the phone has been replaced.* **Mrs Lyons** *exits*]

Act 5, scene 4

The Mother *enters and takes over the phone.*

The Mother: Mickey was here, Linda . . . looking for our Sammy. But Sammy was out . . .

Linda: Mam . . . listen, listen . . . he's going after Eddie.

The Mother: Eddie who?

Linda: Know Eddie who Mickey always used to knock around with . . . He's gone after him. Mam, he's going to do something. I'm terrified . . .

Act 5, scene 5

Narrator:
There's a full moon shining on a hole in the clay
Only black cards dealt on the thirteenth day.
Two spoons in a cup and an itching knee
Oh Jesus shine your light on me
Oh Jesus shine your light on me.

[**Eddie** *leads* **Mickey** *into his house*]

Eddie: Come in, come in. It's terrific to see you, Mickey. Sit down, sit down. Will you have a drink?

Mickey: No. I've had loads.

Eddie: Ah well erm . . .

Mickey: I've been with our Sammy. Remember our Sammy?

Eddie: Yes of course. How is he?

Mickey: How is he? [*Laughs*] He's OK. He was going to come up here with me. But he couldn't. He's working tonight.

Eddie: Ah really. What does he do?

Mickey: He robs! [**Eddie** *unsure but laughing*] Like you do!

Eddie: Pardon.

Mickey: You robbed my missis!

Eddie: Mickey, what's going on?

Mickey: Oh I'll tell you. I'll tell you what's going on! [*He produces a gun*] Our Sammy lent me this. It's the real thing, you know. He's moved on from air pistols. [*Pause*] Know why I borrowed this, Eddie? Mm?

Eddie: [*Moving*] Mickey, I think . . .

Mickey: [*Shrieking and stopping him in his tracks*] Don't you move! [*Pause*] Everything I thought was mine . . . is yours. Is there anything in my life that isn't controlled by you, Eddie?

Eddie: Mickey, all I've tried to do is help. Linda and I, we're not, I just took her out occasionally. Tried to cheer her up.

Mickey: Thanks. Thanks. You do everything for me don't you, Eddie. Well thanks! You've got the power . . . and the control and you do all these things *for me*. [*Pause*] Well why didn't I have any power . . . any control?

Eddie: Look, Mickey . . .

Mickey: No! You look . . . cause I've got the power now. [*Waving the gun*] This says I have. Move over there. [*He does so*] Now move across there. [*He does do*] Now over there . . . and there . . . And put your hands up!

Eddie: Don't you think you should put that thing away Mickey?

Mickey: [*Shouting*] Don't you move! [*Pause*] How does it

feel Eddie? You're not in control now are you? I am! [*Pause*]
I thought my job was mine; but it's not; you fixed it up. My
house. It's not mine. You did it. My wife. Even Linda's not
mine. My son, does he belong to you as well?

Eddie: Mickey!

Mickey: I should shoot you, Eddie, do you know that. I
should shoot you. But I know I won't. Because even with
this ... even holding this to your head, I'm still not in
control of anything, am I? I don't have any power, do I?

Eddie: [*Afraid*] I ... I don't know, Mickey.

Mickey: [*Pause*] Don't you? I do. It's not even a real gun,
Eddie! It's a model, a fake. You couldn't shoot nothing with
it! [*Holds it out as if to fire at* **Eddie**] Look!

[**The Mother** *bursts into the scene. She screams at*
Mickey]

The Mother: Mickey! Don't ... Don't kill him!

Mickey: [*Laughing*] It's all right, look it's just a ... [*Going
to fire*]

The Mother: Mickey ... don't. He's your brother! [*Nodding*]
Yes. You were twins.

[*The two of them looking at her*]

[**Mrs Lyons** *enters with gun*]

Mrs Lyons: You told them. I knew you would. You're a
witch. But you see, it didn't come true. I'll still have
Edward.

[*She goes to shoot* **Mickey**. **Eddie** *screams 'Mother' as he
runs in front of* **Mickey**. **Eddie** *is shot.* **Mrs Lyons** *pauses
for a moment before turning the gun on* **Mickey**. *They are
both dead*]

Narrator:

So did you ever hear the tale of the Johnston twins
As like each other as two new pins,
How one was kept, one given away
They were born and they died on the self same day.

The end

Follow-up activities

Prediction

To predict is to make an intelligent guess or deduction about something before it happens. During a first reading of this play there are a number of opportunities for prediction exercises. For example, discussion or written 'exercises in anticipation' might take place on page 25 at 'Why don't you take the week off?'; on page 67 when Eddie asks Linda out; at the end when Mickey leaves to find Eddie; and also at each age change.

Discussion

1   Talk about the significance of the title. To what does it refer?

2   On page 14. The narrator describes Mrs Johnston as 'That woman, with a stone in place of a heart.' Do you think this is true, or is she just a victim of circumstances?

3   On page 14. Mrs Johnston is quick to use romantic clichés –

> 'He said my eyes were deep blue pools
> My skin as soft as snow
> He told me I was sexier
> Than Marilyn Monroe'

List any other romantic clichés (phrases that are so over used that they lose their impact) you know. You could make them into a short poem, and end the poem with a comment about the clichés.

4   What other options did Mrs Johnston have at the beginning of the play? Who has most freedom of choice?

5   Why is Mrs Lyons so desperate for a child? Discuss the issues of surrogate parenthood: should you be able to buy a child? What if you can give that child a better home than its real parents? What do you think about bringing children from third world countries to be adopted in the affluent west? Should people make money by selling children? Is the public money spent on research into infertility justified (especially in an overpopulated world)?

6   Examine the character of Mrs Lyons. How does she change? Is there any evidence that the author wants us to sympathize with her?

7   Discuss the character of Mrs Johnston. To what extent is she merely a representative of a class or group? (Note that the stage directions simply refer to her as The Mother.) What are her reasons for giving up the baby?

8   How many people in the play can be said to be victims?

9   On page 20 the Mother says 'But like they say at the Welfare, kids can't live on love alone.' Do you think love can completely make up for a lack of money in a home? Can money compensate for a lack of love?

10 On page 23, why does Mrs Lyons say that she wants to do the shopping from now on?

11 Re-read the first encounter between the boys (page 31). How is the contrast in their background reflected in language and attitudes?

12 Discuss the irony of Mrs Johnston's saying on page 37 '. . . you're not the same as him'.

13   On page 37 Mrs Lyons forbids Eddie to play with
     Mickey. Earlier (page 35) Mrs Johnston has done the
     same thing. Is there any difference in their motives?
     'You must understand, it's for your own good. It's only
     because I love you Edward.' Is this justification true?
     How should a loving parent act in such circumstances?
     Why do the two mothers treat their children so
     differently? Which is the better mother? How does each
     mother try to please Edward (see pages 44–5)? What
     motivates each one?

14   Explain why the policewoman takes a different attitude
     to each woman (page 42). Does this happen often?

Education and adolescence

1   a   Why does Mrs Lyons send Eddie to public school?
    b   Brainstorm (i.e. in two minutes, pupils note down as
        many thoughts and ideas of their own) on different
        aspects of state and private education e.g. traditions,
        class size, facilities, etc.
    c   Should a choice of schools be available for all? For
        example, should boarding schools be open to those
        who cannot now afford them?
    d   If all pupils went to state schools would parents of
        those previously in private education demand better
        provisions?
    e   Do public schools give you a 'social leg up'?
    f   Do you think parents send their children to them to
        prevent them from mixing with undesirable pupils?

2   What do you think are the key influences on character –
    heredity, background, education, friends?

3   Mickey hates the boredom of work but prefers it to the
    indignity of unemployment. Do you share this attitude?

4   Re-read the bottom of page 51. 'I'll tell you what I wanna
    do Linda ...'. Discuss adolescent worries. Imagine
    Mickey wrote to a problem page for advice. What would

he say in his letter? Write the reply he would have received.

Characters and relationships

1   On page 58 how does Eddie feel about Linda? Why does he help bring Mickey and Linda together?

2   Why has Mickey's attitude changed by page 62? Is he right to blame Eddie? Has Eddie remained younger than Mickey; if so, why?

3   Re-read page 66 'Eddie, we've been tryin' to get moved for five years. You fix it up in five minutes!' Eddie, like Mrs Lyons, is able to cut through official channels to arrange things (see page 22 where Mrs Lyons says 'Certificates can be arranged. I can pay.'). Do you think this happens a great deal? Should it happen? If it shouldn't, how could it be stopped? Can you understand Mickey's attitude when he finds out? Do you sympathize more with Mickey or with Eddie and Linda?

4   Re-read what The Mother as narrator says on page 67. Discuss women's role, and marriage. How similar is Linda's experience of marriage to Mrs Johnston's? Is she justified in seeing Eddie?

5   On page 71, Mickey says 'Why didn't I have any power ... any control?' Is this true? If it is what caused it?

6   Do certain names (for example Darren Wayne and Donna Marie) reflect social class? If so, why?

7   How many people in the class are superstitious? Make a list of superstitions. Which superstitions do even the non-superstitious observe? Why do we have superstitions? There are many examples of superstitions in *Blood Brothers*.

   a   Why does Mrs Lyons make up the superstition about twins? (see page 27)

   b   How does her attitude to this superstition change throughout the play?

    c   How does this superstition affect the rest of the play?

    d   This superstition turned out to be true. Does this mean that the ending was 'fated'?

    e   What other superstitions can you find in *Blood Brothers* and what effect do they have on the play?

8   Throughout *Blood Brothers* there are ironic twists; characters say and do things which are intended to produce one effect and they have the opposite outcome.

    a   How does Eddie's act of kindness in finding Mickey work in the factory have the opposite effect from the one Eddie intended? (see page 65)

    b   Could the outcome have been avoided?

    c   What other ironic twists can you find in *Blood Brothers*?

    d   Why do you think the author put these ironic twists in the play?

9   Which characters do you like most? Give reasons for your answer.

10   Which stages of life are we shown in the play? Why are those particular ones chosen? Compare your own life at each of the stages so far. Which do you think are the key stages of your life?

11   Find ways in which the relationship between the twins parallels that of the mothers, e.g. the swearing of an oath, Eddie offering Mickey money, Eddie arranging things.

12   This play makes a statement about contrasting ways of life. Do you like plays to have a message or do you think they should just entertain?

Improvisation

(Each of these scenes may be improvised.)

1 A radio or TV interview with Mrs Lyons and Mrs Johnston.
2 Teatime at each household when the boys are aged about seven.
3 An extra scene at the end of the play.

Drama

Improvise or rehearse the trial of Mrs Lyons. You will need to cast parts, and have two or three people as lawyers for both the defence and the prosecution as well as one (or possibly three) people as the judge. The remainder of the class form the jury. The characters will need time to look back over the play to focus on what they did and said while the defence and prosecution draw up a list of questions for the witnesses and the accused. The judge will announce the order that witnesses are called in, and s/he will also make notes for a summing up to the jury at the end of the trial. The jury should elect a foreperson, but each member of the jury should also keep notes so that they can justify their decision at the end of the trial.

It is best to arrange parts in the lesson before the one in which the trial is held, and to hear the jury's verdict in the lesson after the trial.

Before the trial you could go through the police file – see writing idea number 13 on page 81.

Writing

1 One in seventy births are of twins. There are fraternal and identical twins, and there have been examples of special communication between twins. If you are not a twin invent a twin for yourself. Describe his or her character.
2 Make a diagram of the way the twins in *Blood Brothers* move away from each other. Start with them being at the same point at birth. Notice that at certain times they will come closer together.

3   List the times that Eddie helps Mickey. How does he help? Are there any times when Mickey helps Eddie?

4   List the ways in which each boy's life is like that of his mother e.g. Mickey has to get married, is old before his time, is in danger of losing his partner to a younger (but similar) rival.

5   Write a newspaper report following the shooting. Give all the main details of the story in the first paragraph. Decide on your headline after you have written the article.

N.B. You could write one report for a popular paper which would be short and quite sensational, and one for a quality newspaper which would go into more detail. (Before doing this compare the treatment of a real story in a popular and quality paper.) You could make one of your reports sympathetic to Mrs Lyons and the other sympathetic to Mrs Johnston.

6   Describe a visit to Mrs Johnston's house and a contrasting visit to Mrs Lyons. Focus in particular on the living rooms and on the contrasting appearance of the two women. You could design film sets for the houses and costumes for the women.

7   In both the Johnston and the Lyons households the husbands are absent. Contrast the reasons for their absence. What are the differences and similarities in the effect that this has on the wives? You have a little information about the two husbands – use what you can infer to write a character study of each of them.

8   List the advantages and disadvantages of being a member of each family.

9   Imagine that in their first year of secondary school both Eddie and Mickey have been asked to describe their home. Write their descriptions keeping in mind the type of language each would use.

10 Write Eddie and Mickey's school reports at the ages of

8, 11 and 16. Keep in the mind the different types of school they attended. For the secondary school reports select three major subjects to write about as well as the form tutor's general report.

11 Imagine that the two boys change places for a day. Write Eddie's description of Mickey's home and school and vice versa.

12 Write Mickey and Eddie's obituaries.

13 Compile the police file which is opened on the murders. It will consist of a number of documents: a description of the scene of the crime; statements from Mrs Lyons and Mrs Johnston; brief details about each of the deceased; charge sheet. This would be a useful basis for a trial – see Drama ideas above.

14 Imagine you are a journalist and write a day in the life of either Eddie, Mickey or Linda.

15 Design a poster to attract foster parents for Eddie when he was just a baby.

16 Write from your own experience about either forbidden things in childhood, or childhood pranks or misunderstandings.

Structure

1 The play is a musical. How would you stage the songs and dances?

2 The play itself is like a ballad: the narrator's opening speech is in ballad form; it tells a story; it is meant to entertain and inform; the events are larger than life; and it has a strong formal organization.

3 The characters and events are realistic but the style of the play frequently reminds us that what we are watching is not real. Why do you think Willy Russell decided to use music? Look at each of the songs and say what they add to the drama.

4 The play also has elements of melodrama: strong

emotion, sensational events, punishment for guilt. Look for examples.

5   Look at the opening scenes (pages 14–17). How is the song used to give background information? Why do the cast change roles?

6   Examine how the theme of dancing or waltzing recurs through the play.

7   In what ways is the play suited to being performed by a school?

8   Why is a narrator used?

9   How realistic is the ending? Could it have ended differently? How?

10   Other ways of dealing with the themes of separated twins or of children given away include:

> *Rumpelstiltskin*
> *The Comedy of Errors*
> *The Caucasian Chalk Circle*
> *Midnight's Children*